T0128527

Emotion
Etched in Words

A collection of Poems and Love Letters

B. L. Fleming

authorHOUSE®

AuthorHouse™
1663 Liberty Drive
Bloomington, IN 47403
www.authorhouse.com
Phone: 1-800-839-8640

Published by AuthorHouse   04/19/2012

ISBN: 978-1-4685-8815-6 (sc)
ISBN: 978-1-4685-8814-9 (hc)
ISBN: 978-1-4685-8813-2 (e)

Library of Congress Control Number: 2012907224

Any people depicted in stock imagery provided by Thinkstock are models, and such images are being used for illustrative purposes only.
Certain stock imagery © Thinkstock.

This book is printed on acid-free paper.

Contents

Dedications

To My Mother, Mary Louise Hill Fleming who took the time to make me understand that education and determination are the keys to achieving any goal you set your mind to.

To the Kids, Carrington and Candace. You two changed my life so much for the better and I have never looked back! You will never know just how much Daddy loves you and thanks you both for all that you have grown to be.

To My Inspiration Nation: To every friend and acquaintance that encouraged me to write and publish this collection of my emotions and feelings this is for all of your. I sincerely hope you enjoy reading it as much as I have enjoyed writing it.

Special thanks to the following

Tonya (Toni) Johnson: Thank you for believing in me and for the never ending friendship. Above all thank you for all of the smiles and laughter.

Pamela Prosper: You always have so many kind and positive words. The sayings you write inspire me so much. Thank You. I sincerely hope you consider publishing your own book! I am saving you a seat on the book tour.

Ava Walker: All those late nights staying up and reading these writings online then encouraging me to continue. Here is the finished result! Thank You!

Valerie Burley: Thank you for pushing me forward in this dream. One day I am going to write a book about all of our exploits from the college days!

Rebecca Salazar: Who would have thought that a late nite game of UNO would lead to such a friendship. Thank you for all the encouragement.

Regina Cloud Ward: What can I say, your smiling face and wit inspired so much of what I have written in the last year. I'm sure this book would be completely different without your influence. Thank you so much . . . .

From the time I first took pen in hand and made my first attempt to write a song I have loved creating with words. This is a snapshot of the feelings embedded in my heart, written to share with anyone who wishes to pick up a book and read them. Thank you in advance.

Patrice K. Walker, (Author of "When Water Was Free"), Thank you for being a trailblazer and encouraging me to follow the path laid by you. You are a great friend and an inspiration, I truly love you.

Darlene Bowman. I sincerely hope that one day soon we are sitting across from each other sipping on some Starbucks and writing on an original script for TV! The sky is the limit and you inspire me to see beyond my own dreams. Thank you cousin.

JUST FOR MOTHERS

Thank You Mama

It's been some time now. My how the days have passed

And I remember simple things. Those are the ones that last.

I shall never forget each life lesson You lovingly took time to teach

From how to tie my own shoes to achieving goals that seemed just out of reach

You were never judgmental instead, inspiring and filled with praise

Although I overheard you tell some friends "the boy got some crazy ways!"

But stand behind me, yes that you did do

Mama, I hope you realize the greatest inspiration I ever had is you

And with these memories sometimes I have to hold back a tear

But that's only because Dear God I wish you were here!

Yet before that first teardrop hits the ground

I can feel the light from your smile and your love all around

and the sadness I felt starts to turn to great joy

as I hear a voice deep within say

"You're still Mama's Big Boy"

A Mother's Love

A Mother's Love is cherished
much more than diamonds and gold
For without a Mother's love
this world can seem unbearable and cold.
A Mother's love exists, unconditional
and without bounds.
And yes in a good man
a great Mother's love is found
Now Fathers are great too
but a man must know his place
For when we find ourselves troubled
We long for our Mother's embrace!
So Sons and Daughters go forth
seek your Mothers wherever the place
Hold Her, Squeeze Her! And bring a smile upon her face.
Tell Her just how much you care
and love her in every way
For we are not promised tomorrow
So please! Please tell her today!

Reach for the Sky

My Mother always taught me to hold my head up high

for dreams I held inside were as vast as God's bright sky

and anything in life I really wanted to achieve

first and foremost in Myself, She said I must believe

So each and every night as She lay me down to dream

She told me "reach forever toward your goals, though hard it
*   sometimes seems"*

And I owe that woman a bill I shall never be able to repay

She deserves year round adulation! Much more than just one day!

WORDS OF LOVE

More than merely words

You say I write such sweet things about you.
The truth and reality is simple:
The eloquence with which I write is driven
by my overwhelming desire to know
exactly where I reside within
the bounds of your heart.

The Very First Look

When I first looked upon your face
I recognized your beauty
When I heard you speak,
I marveled at your intelligence
When I watch as you laugh
I share in your joy
When I hold you as you cry
I feel your pain
When you lift my spirit
I experience your caring
When you share with me your dreams
I glance inside your heart
Every time you say you love me
I realize You are God's blessing
And above all when I look in your eyes
I see my future
Were I to awaken without you in my world;
that I simply refuse to imagine.

My Prayer for You

I'm not usually one to fumble and stumble over words
when I have something to say
But it seems every time we have a chance to speak I find
myself wondering if what I said came out OK
It's not that I feel intimidated or nervous when I'm around you
Maybe it's the fact that your are so special I'm just in awe
of all you do
Now don't laugh at me, though I so love to see that
sensational smile
Just know I dream of a day I can tell you everything you are
in my heart and that will take awhile
Yes I'm sure you're smiling that beautiful smile as my world
just got Oh So Bright!
So these will be my final words. My Dear I wish you all you pray
and please have a spectacular night.

Daydreams

Eyes that tell of distant places. Fun filled dreams dripping with happiness. A smile that illuminates a darkened room from corner to corner and warms a cold winter's nite. Just being near you is like being embraced by a friendly blanket you've known for years cuddling you in your favorite chair as you reminisce on comforting thoughts of blissful encounters. This is what I'm thinking when I sit and smile for hours at a time, the joy of having you on my mind.

Shining Smile

In everything you do your smile comes shining through
a walking testament to God who truly adores you
You brighten my day and if I can only watch from afar
please remember you are thought of fondly, always, Wherever you are
And anytime you glance in that mirror and fail to find your smile
just give me a call I'll be there . . . . no matter how many the miles
So if you're smiling now my job right here is done
not the ending that I seek but yes a small battle won
So take a deep breath now and release it with a sigh!
And know these feelings in my heart are never meant to die.

Our Whispers

*I whisper your name into the wind and no matter where
you are you hear the gentle sound of my voice. You can't
contain the smile that gently moves across your face knowing
just how much I long to feel your arms around me and that
comforting approval. You try to resist the urge to answer but
slowly give in to the temptation to speak. As my name flows
across your lips I hear it and at once know I have truly found
my soulmate as we have a bond born in heaven announced
out loud and carried on the wings of angels*

The Moment

Your face, like the morning sun, slowly washes away
the darkness, and as the night fades gently away your smile
radiant and aglow, shines upon me warming my very
soul to a point where I am overcome with the joy of being
within your aura. As I look deeply into your tantalizing eyes
I realize you are gazing back at me in the very same way. In
that very moment I knew this was love . . . .

So Close

I passed in close proximity to my
Angel today.
It was exciting to know She was near as I passed
along the way
See She's like a comet passing ever closer to Earth
illuminating the sky
I wondered if she felt me too; did I brighten her day
as I slowly drove on by.
I hunger for the day She and I can sit
and just talk for awhile
Simply to laugh, yes to cry, or maybe
just to share a smile
Until that day I shall simply sit
be patient and wait
For She knows the desires of my heart
and that's not up for debate
So if you glance My way and catch me
smiling for no apparent reason
It's because I know a wondrous Love
is coming into season.

When did We Meet

Did we ever chase fireflies as darkness slowly overcame the light
did we play basketball, hide and seek or have a pillow fight
I can't remember exactly when or how we met,
I only know it's you I choose never to forget.
Have we held hands at dusk and slowly walked along the beach
or pushed each other toward goals we thought we'd never reach.
Have we sought each other all this time and really didn't see
Together we are stronger! Not You and I; but We!
I pray that our tomorrows are filled with joyous memories of today
and I guess these words I write are really meant to say . . . .
I can't remember exactly when or how we met
I only know it's Us I choose never to forget . . . .

Answered Prayers

I asked God for an Angel and He showed me your sweet smile
I asked for love deep as the oceans, He said
"Walk with Me for awhile".
I asked Him for my crowning jewel
He put Your name upon my mind
then whispered to my spirit
"No greater love shall you find.
And since you both choose to place Me
first within your lives,
Sit back, be now patient as
soon your time arrives".
So here I sit still and patient, with this
smile across my face
for His promise is that soon,
I shall know your warm embrace
I'll call your name upon the wind
you'll respond to me in smiles
For he answered both our prayers
when We walked with Him awhile . . . .

Oceans Apart

It's hard being this close to a dream but still oceans apart
That's why this time I reach not with my hands but with words
from my heart
The adulation I feel grows stronger with each passing Day
Emotions, hard to hide surface and yet reality continues
to sweep you away.
We speak briefly, parting way to soon leaving me feeling aghast
I sit and wonder in comfortless isolation
why our conversations didn't last.
Just as I'm ready to give up and throw in the towel
you appear again, flashing that heartfelt and
effortless smile.
So here we go again, I stand before you quite smitten
And once again I'll try and sway you with these unfeigned
words I have written.

Sweet Lullabies

Reach inside my crying eyes
sing me to sleep sweet lullabies
and touch my soul with dreams so true
in a world where there's only me and you
and if and when that sun does rise
these dreams of you they must subside
I choose to sleep and dream of you
for my world without you just won't do . . .

My Vow

You are sincerely the one thing
with which I cannot live without
It is no doubt you were sent to me
to bring a positive change about.
And I so hope that in some small way
I've touched your soul leading us here today
So before our friends I appear on bended knee
I offer you my life and I want the world to see
Let me simply say this is only the start
From this day forward only you shall retain my heart
As surely as in this moment two become as one,
I promise to cherish every breath we share,
until time itself is done.

Loves Embrace

Shadows of intimate embraces
projected on the wall by the light
of an almost spent candle.
Sensuous sounds of passion fill
the fragrant air of a room where
in a moment of unadulterated
affection two have become one.
All of this anchored by a Love
representing the desires of two
souls brought together
under God's guidance
Joined in His presence
and adorned in matrimony.
Til death do they part!

LOVE LETTERS

Anxious

Anxiously we reach with words cultivated in our hearts.
So wanting an chance to convert each phrase into an action
to arouse an emotional response intended for that particular
chosen one. The riposte; Silence: A deafening silence heard
not by ears but piercing one's soul to never imagined depths.
Such Silence effecting a hasty retreat to place of sanctuary
where you are no longer vulnerable. And you speak no more.

The Proposal

I'm not really sure where it all started or if time itself has any bearing on just how I feel.

I have realized that each time I look at you I am drawn ever closer to your very essence.

I long to know what fills the inner corners of your heart. I have come to know the cover

of the book so well but have glanced at but a few pages inside, still Your story is as alluring

as your smile that warms the center of my soul. Your eyes filled with the joy of knowing God

and rallying to serve His purpose for You in life. Words of wisdom and caring flow across your

lips to those in need of comfort or reassuring. You are a rare and beautiful flower complete and

polished like a diamond that emerges from the depths of the Earth to sparkle and shine. You

are to be adorned and placed upon a pedestal. The crowning jewel itself promised to a Godly

man, not to complete him but to enhance his very being.

Take my hand and walk with me. Allow me to show the world I have indeed found my "Good

Thing" promised by God, sought by many and claimed by few. Share my world where you shall

be Queen and treated accordingly. Where comfort awaits you in time of need. Where we can

Love, Laugh and Live under God's direction. Where when He Himself looks upon us He says,

"It is Good".

A Note of Love

I awakened today to the sheer radiance of your face laying next to me.
A smile that rivals the sun itself in brightness. Our breathing
appearing
to be one. I slowly opened my eyes from a sleep that had lasted way
to long, A sleep that removed me from the reality of you. For no dream
I can conjure in my mind could ever compare to the joy the mere
presence of you brings my heart. You are undoubtedly the foremost
reason I choose to awaken each and every day for you are the total
fulfillment of everything I have ever asked God for in a Friend, a
Companion, Lover and a Wife. Thank you for being all that you are.
Words cannot begin to describe all that you mean to me. Just know
that every time I smile it is a reflection of the way you make me feel.
My heart cannot contain the love inside intended for you alone. If you
ever ask me to place a number on how much I love you I would start
by
counting each and every grain of sand on every beach on Earth then
multiply that by the number of stars shining throughout the universe.
Still that number would pale in comparison to the love I feel each time
I look into your eyes. The debt I owe the Lord for placing you in my
life can never be repaid. I can only do as He commands and love You
as Jesus loved the Church. Please place this small token of my love
somewhere in your heart in the file phrased "I love You" because I
promise, I do . . . .

The Walk

I Long to slowly walk along the beach with you, the sun slowly setting as the waves gently brush against our feet We stroll hand in hand, entwined in each others smiles. Oblivious to all that surrounds us. We are in stride together in precise time supporting each other as we move along in the moist path. The sweet smell of fresh ocean air invigorates our minds stimulating the ever growing feelings of trust and comfort between us. The moonlight gradually replaces the day but the twinkle of the stars cannot compare to the alluring sparkle in your eyes for it is in them where I see my future, our future. Sheer happiness and bliss await! We are eagerly engaged in conversation sharing hopes

and dreams wishes and prayers, The chill of the night
fills the air and we take a seat on a log wrapping in
a blanket arm in arm near a small fire. We draw ever
closer as the hours slip away. Mind body and soul our
hearts begin to beat as one in rhythm like the melody
of a sweet and memorable love song. We watch as
the embers from the fire drift slowly into the night sky.
We share a soft and romantic kiss and I realize I have
been searching for you for all my life and I never want
to let you go . . . At last you and I are one . . . . The sun
slowly rises opposite of where we watched it escape
from view hours ago . . . as I contemplate my prayer
is a simple one . . . . to do this all over again
forever.

Adrift in Memories

We set sail slowly drifting on this ship of love filled with precious

memories as far as our eyes can reach. We inhale seas of calm blue
   water

reflecting the vision of scattered clouds and bright sunshine aglow
   upon

the water. Ripples on the surface exaggerate my smile stretching it
   from

ear to ear as I think of you and adventures yet to come. Where do we go

from here? It really doesn't matter for it is the journey that I love!

Traces

I think back and remember traces of faces and smiles gone by
looking out over a crowd and wondering why
It seems that I spend way too much time thinking if I should try
or would it end as always, a pleasant hello then just goodbye.
But this time was different or did my ears lie? . . .
You were much more than pleasant when you
smiled and said hi!
But alas I remembered,
traces of faces and memories gone by,
so this latest encounter ends with a sigh . . . .
now I find myself walking away and wondering why,
what would have happened if I just once more did try . . . .

A Thanks for Grace

I bet you didn't know it's true
but behind that smile you thought you knew
Once lived a heart that hurt at times
but God brought me through to a place divine.
Now when you look upon my face
that shines because of His love and Grace
Understand with all that I've been through
He made me smile by sending you . . . .

IN NEED OF LOVE

True Beauty

I sometimes sit and wonder why
some appear more pleasing to the eye
Yet as we take time to look within
it is there where true beauty begins
So why not all just close our eyes
and not dwell on smiles that bring disguise
Try listening for a heart that's true
For there real love waits for you.

Laughter In My Tears

If you see me crying please be not sad nor fear,
for when you see those raindrops fall
there's laughter in every tear
When I cry because I'm sad
there are memories to ease my woe
For you see tears, like rain, loosen up our soil
and allow us each to grow.
Now go enjoy every smile I bring
and my weeping do not fear
For the most beautiful smiles I've ever found
have followed painful tears.

Weary

Wearily I wait, tired form the battle.
The will to continue flows heavily through
my veins with each and every heartbeat. and yet
the strength to continue is diminished with
each breath I secure.
Slowly night overcomes the day and
like an artist's paint brush each stroke
paints the canvas darker and darker
until the light is no more.
Love you have rescued
Me time and time
yet I can not feel you
near so in anguish I wait.

Far too long it has been
since I felt your warm embrace
that smile that warms my inner
being, hidden from view behind
unrelenting clouds.
The night, the darkness
consume me as I slowly
melt into the never ending
abyss! Oh Joy where
are you?

B. L. Fleming

Of Loss

*The night so eerily still as I lay here in darkened silence
encompassed in broken dreams and failed expectations.
The blame, mine and mine alone; for two had a dream
that one chose to shatter. Lies and deceit only bring
conclusion to hopes as it erodes faith and cancels elation.
The conclusion; Death to a relationship once filled with
the brilliance and merriment. Memories once cherished
dissolve into indifference with their final destination
being the void of loves lost and forgotten. Yet it is said
that love forgives all in time and the hope should be for
a reuniting of friends though the passion once remarkable,
shall never be rekindled to the grandeur once achieved
so easily by two.*

Envy

With eyes of envy, why do you covet
what you think you see in me?
A jealous heart clouds your judgment,
Truth is "you" is all "you" need to be.
Invidious words fill your heart, soul and mind
but only pain is returned
and that, soon you shall find.
Malicious lies, falsehoods . . . .
words filled with so much hate,
All spoken by you . . . .
Me meant to berate.
Like the old saying goes
"words can't hurt me"
Glance in the mirror
There the one destroyed
you will see!!

INSPIRATION

My Dreams Your Plan

I had big dreams for my life, yours were larger! I had lofty ambition and goals

Your path led me higher. When I fall I know your Mercy. When I'm obedient

I know your Grace. When I say thank you for loving me Lord you reply, "It

could never be any other way"!

Patience

There is a road less traveled that leads to enduring adulation and joy.
That road is called Patience. Patience will lead you to a life adorned
in happiness and fulfillment. Yes true happiness is found at an address
on Patience Road. There you no longer have to settle for less than you
and yours are entitled to. True Love and True Happiness live side by
side
on Patience Road. During your travels along Patience Road you are
sure
to encounter a much needed traveling companion named Wisdom.
Embrace
Wisdom. Learn from Wisdom for Wisdom knows the address of True
Love
and True Happiness. Always travel Patience Road always travel with
Wisdom.

Know No Weakness

My Father knows no weakness
He is what makes me strong
I'm built on his foundation
Therefore I shall never stand alone
Before you bring slander against me
understand it is He who in my heart resides
All things you say against me
yes in Him I shall confide.
Please know I wish to you
no adversity or harm
But when you speak against His Children
You're the source of your own storm!

Goals

Not ultimately reaching the first dream does not diminish the lessons learned as you follow the path. It is not that you are a failure just the dream you were pursuing was not meant to be yours. Grasp Life's lessons! Move ever forward and continue to focus on the unsurpassed prize that remains yours and yours alone/

The Light

I was afraid of the dark until I came to know You Lord.
For You are the Light and the Way.
No matter how hard darkness fights
it without fail starts to fade with the first
rays of the morning sun.
I realize within your assurance
I am forever safe.
For there is nothing that manifest itself in the dark
that You Lord cannot see.

As the Earth Cries

Silently she cries
injured through
years of abuse.
Wasteful and ignorant
we continue to choose
Convenience over conservation
mindlessly we use
Resources irreplaceable
What else can she do!
She tries in vain to warn us as
She shakes trembles and cries
But to those who would listen
the leaders tell them lies
Her impatience is growing
We must heed her call!
Or I fear it is Us
Mankind who will fall!

Again of Love

It's nearly three in the morning and suddenly I find myself wide awake. An overwhelming desire to just watch you sleep, such a joy your presence brings me. I quietly open the blinds so the moonlight shines along your body and comes to a sparkling nuance as it gently meets your face. That Angelic face, so bright and filled with merriment, beautiful and alluring as a song set to a memorable melody . . . . One you hear over and over in your mind smiling as you hum along. I think to myself "Oh what have I done to deserve you?" Will the waking of the morning sun find this to be only a dream. Then I feel you take my hand in yours and pull me ever closer. I struggle in the moment to find words to exclaim my adulation for you but before I can speak words flow from your heart and gently pass your lips meeting my ears as you say "can you just hold me like this forever

Where do I Start

Oh my! I'm not really sure where to start

how do you tell someone they hold the key to your heart

It's not like it started yesterday but very long ago

the thoughts were there but the words, . . . I just didn't know

In school you loved me, . . . said I was like your big brother

And Yes I shed a tear as you proclaimed love for another.

But there were great times! we were always good friends . . .

You fell a . . . sleep in my arms crying cause some new love had come to an end.

I'd hold you and rock you, whisper in your ear and say

"Don't worry sweetheart, someone special will come and love you some day."

That always caused you to smile and made me feel good too

Oh why! Couldn't I just say that my whole world revolved around you!

Time passed we raised families, they grew up and moved away

and still I had thoughts of being your special someone some day.

We're both single now and it feels like it's finally time

let me sit down and see if the right words I can find

I'll start by saying I've loved you for so long

If I were a musician, yes, ... I'd write you a song

Beautiful words fill my head ready to flow through my pen

A Shortness of breath! No! Not Now Lord! I'm about to begin!

Yes these are my thoughts just a few words more!

But the light grows dim as I fall to the floor.

Now tears fill my paper where words should have been

Oh Why did I wait so long to begin!

I'm looking down from high above now. Oh My is that me!

People filing by now others not wanting to see.

Oh but there she is I knew she'd come by

She stops and smiles trying so hard not to cry

Then she exclaims: "Oh My! I wish I knew where to start

but how do I say you hold the keys to my heart.

You see it started so very long ago

feelings were there but words I just didn't know.

You held me close and I waited for you to say:

I'm that someone special who's coming your way . . . . "

Author introduction by Candace Fleming: From the time I was a small child I watched as this man played Guitar, Bass Guitar, Drums and Piano always creating always making his own music.

As I got older I began to read some of the songs and poems he had written as a hobby and listened as family members and friends alike encouraged him to share these with the world. His answer was always the same, "I don't have time right now I'm takning care of these kids and My Mother". Always putting others first is a way of life for him. Now that my Brother, Carrington, is off on his own journey in the United States Air Force and my Grandmother has gone to live with the Angels it came as no surprise to me that my Father said to me, "Baby Girl. I think I'm going to put some of these poems and love letters in a book". I was so excited and pleased that he was choosing to share with anyone that cared to pick up a book what I have seen all my life.

That is a glimpse inside the heart of a gentle, caring man who has so much room for love and is willing to share with the world. I proudly present these works from my Father's heart and soul

"Emotion Etched in Words" by Barry LaMont Fleming . . . . B.L. Fleming. Thank you for reading Candace N. Fleming, April/2012